Original title:
Searching for Meaning with a Side of Fries

Copyright © 2025 Creative Arts Management OÜ
All rights reserved.

Author: Seraphina Caldwell
ISBN HARDBACK: 978-1-80566-256-3
ISBN PAPERBACK: 978-1-80566-551-9

A Tasty Odyssey of Thought

In a diner booth so tight,
I ponder sauce and what is right.
Is ketchup life's true secret spice?
Or is it mustard, oh so nice?

With every bite of greasy cheer,
I chase my dreams both far and near.
Fries like wands that wave in glee,
They point to truths that set me free.

A burger speaks, its wisdom bold,
While onion rings share tales untold.
In each fry, a quest begins,
To find the joy that always wins.

When Life Hands You Fries

Life tossed me fries, oh what a gift,
But where's the meaning? Just a rift.
I crunch on thoughts with every bite,
And wonder, is this wrong or right?

Dipped in mayo, sweet delight,
I contemplate through day and night.
Are golden fries the pot of gold?
Or merely snacks when tempers scold?

I chuckle at the twist of fate,
While munching on my crispy plate.
In every fry, a story shines,
Of messy laughs and secret signs.

Reflecting Over a Basket of Bliss

In a basket, dreams collide,
With salty fries, I take a ride.
Each crispy crunch a fleeting thought,
Tasting wonders that I sought.

Life's a platter, stacked so high,
With veggie tales and apple pie.
But fries, my friend, they steal the show,
With each dip, ideas start to flow.

As mayo swirls in salty pools,
I ponder over all the rules.
Is learning fun? Is wisdom fried?
In every bite, my thoughts reside.

The Side Order of Oversight

I ordered wisdom, hold the fries,
Yet here they come, a sweet surprise.
With every bite, I start to see,
The absent thoughts that used to be.

Like crispy sides, where truths reside,
Each morsel makes me laugh and glide.
On this plate, the world is clear,
With every fry, I shed a tear.

Oh life, you joke, you twist and turn,
In baskets deep, the lessons churn.
Next time I crave a thought that's wise,
I'll just remember, hold the fries.

Gravy Trails and Truths

In a diner booth, I sit and ponder,
Is the secret sauce just magic, I wonder?
With every bite, revelations creep,
Could fries hold wisdom, buried deep?

Ketchup smiles while mustard frowns,
On this plate, the world spins around.
A fork in hand, I muse and chew,
Could crispy bites bring clarity too?

Crispy Cravings

Golden brown, they call my name,
Each crunch a giggle, fries to blame.
With grease as ink, my thoughts take flight,
In every dip, I spark delight.

Potatoes shaped like dreams, oh dear,
What wisdom lies in deep-fried cheer?
Seasoned truths in every layer,
Soggy thoughts? No room for prayer!

Hidden Layers

Under crispy coats, secrets hide,
Between each fry, what dreams collide?
With ranch or cheese, I take a taste,
Could wisdom linger, not to waste?

In this bowl of joy, I take a leap,
Fried hopes float, while sorrows seep.
Laughter dances on parchment paper,
Every bite a joyful caper.

Under the Golden Arches

Beneath a sign that glows so bright,
I search for truths in every bite.
With fries so tempting, I must confess,
Wisdom is wrapped in greasy excess.

A soda pop cheers, my thoughts ogle,
Life's greatest questions under a toggle.
Crispy Laughter, oh how it flies,
In paper wrappers, the truth lies.

A Journey in Oil and Sorrow

In a fryer's embrace, I start to dive,
Searching for meaning, feeling alive.
On a platter, my hopes start to sizzle,
In each greasy bite, emotions drizzle.

So come join me in this funny quest,
To find the joy that fries manifest.
With laughter sprinkled like salt on fries,
I figure it out, under boundless skies.

An Exploration of Comfort Food

In the kitchen I do dwell,
Potato slices, fry them well.
A crunch, a bite, where's the rest?
Happiness served, I feel blessed.

A burger joins, a classic feast,
Can't stop eating, I'm the beast.
Ketchup rivers, mustard flows,
Saucy dreams, where pleasure grows.

A slice of pie, a scoop of ice,
Calories hidden, who needs advice?
With every bite, I find the bliss,
In every meal, I can't resist.

Laughter bubbles, joy's a friend,
With every fry, I'll ascend.
Dancing fries on my plate,
In this banquet, it's never late.

Frying Away the Uncertainty

In a pot of boiling fate,
Drop those fries—don't hesitate!
Crispy echoes, hint of doubt,
With each crunch, I scream and shout.

Life's a burger, messy, fun,
Onions flying—who's got a gun?
Pickles dancing, relish grins,
In this chaos, laughter wins.

A milkshake swirls, sweet delight,
Is that joy or just a bite?
With whipped cream, I start to dream,
Amid the fries, I find my theme.

Bite the chaos, fry the pain,
With every crunch, I bounce back again.
The golden comfort on my plate,
Tastes like freedom—I can't wait!

Fryer's Insight

In the kitchen, dreams may fry,
Dancing shadows as time slips by.
Oil bubbles with a cheesy grin,
What's the secret? Let the feast begin.

Salted thoughts, they sparkle bright,
Crispy questions in the moonlight.
Dipping sauces like theories bold,
With each taste, new wonders unfold.

The Search for Lost Flavor

Once a slice, now a fable told,
Crisp adventures, never grow old.
Searching spice where ketchup flows,
In every bite, a story grows.

Flickering lights on tater skins,
Silly thoughts and smiling grins.
Through the grease, let laughter seep,
In this quest, our hearts we keep.

Bites of Wisdom

Potato wisdom on my plate,
In each crunch, no room for hate.
Funny thoughts in every bite,
Fries and puns, pure delight!

Starch and jest, a perfect blend,
No deep-fried question we can't mend.
With each dip, let laughter grow,
In this banquet of joy, let's go!

Beyond the Grease

Underneath the sizzling dome,
Lies a world far from home.
Crispy dreams float in the air,
With every fry, love and care.

Under forks that never tire,
Chasing giggles, never higher.
Through the salt, a truth reveals,
In the crunch, our joy appeals.

Drizzle and Dilemma

In the diner, thoughts collide,
Ketchup rivers, feelings slide.
Mustard whispers from the jar,
What does it mean to be a star?

Napkins flutter like lost dreams,
Fries and giggles, silly schemes.
I ponder life with every bite,
Drowned in sauce, is this delight?

Sentiments with a Dash of Spice

On the grill, my heart does sizzle,
Salted wounds, but still I drizzle.
A sprinkle here, a dash of cheer,
Do potatoes hold my deepest fear?

With each crunch, I taste the jest,
Life's a fryer; I'm on a quest.
Spicy thoughts stir up bright moods,
Amid the fries, I find my foods.

Chasing Happiness in Greasy Trails

Grease stains map my way around,
Happiness lost, but fries abound.
With each dip, I ponder fate,
Is joy just crunch or is it great?

I chase that flavor, quest absurd,
Laughter bubbles, barely heard.
In this world of savory moans,
Are we but spuds with bumpy bones?

The Snack Shack of Self

In the snack shack, souls collide,
Fries and wisdom, side by side.
Burgers bounce with thoughts so wild,
Are we just comfort's hungry child?

With dipping sauce, I take a leap,
In crispy bites, my secrets seep.
Life's a platter, served with glee,
I find myself with calorie.

Forking into the Unknown

In the diner booth I sit, just my fries and me,
A crispy sidekick to ponder life's mystery.
Ketchup cascades like dreams on my plate,
But can it help define my real fate?

The fork in hand, I poke and prod,
Is this deep thought or just a food facade?
A salty crunch to soothe a fraying mind,
Maybe wisdom lurks in seasoning combined.

The Spirit of Snack Time Reflections

A napkin with wisdom, crumbs of delight,
Every fry tells tales beneath the neon light.
Do they have secrets or just a weird texture?
While I dunk and ponder my next big venture.

With every bite, my thoughts start to flow,
Is this a meal or an introspective show?
A shake of salt, a sprinkle of zest,
Perhaps the key to life lies in this quest.

Crisp Edges and Soft Centers

O fries, you bring joy in the crunch and the soft,
With each hypnotic bite, my worries lift off.
The gold beneath the surface, oh so divine,
Unraveling puzzles with each tasty line.

In the haze of grease, do I find my own tale?
Do I care if my journey's riddled with fail?
With grease-stained hands and a heart full of cheer,
I munch on existence, a fry-loving seer.

The Flavor of Identity in Every Bite

Are we mere toppings or zest on a fry?
I ponder this boldly, with sauce on the side.
Renegade potatoes with a story to tell,
In crispy freedom, we shmear and we dwell.

With every flavor, my essence revealed,
Laughter and crunch, my soul is unsealed.
So grab a fried fortune and share it with me,
For identity's twisty like curly fries, you see!

The Ingredient of Existence

In the fryer of life, we all do dwell,
Hoping for answers, as the oil does swell.
Salted and crisped, our thoughts take flight,
What's the secret spice? Could it be delight?

Lettuce and dreams, all tossed in a bowl,
Zesty adventures, are they good for the soul?
With ketchup smirking, we dip and we dive,
Finding our flavor, just trying to survive.

Fries on the Edge of Discovery

Potato-shaped ponderings, golden and bright,
In grease we trust, oh what a sight!
Each fry a question, each crunch a tease,
Do we find answers or just fried peas?

With sprinkles of logic and a dash of cheer,
We munch on our worries, let's toast with a beer!
In the fast lane of thought, we speed up the quest,
For a side of enlightenment, served piping hot, best!

The Aroma of Aspirations

Fragrant dreams waft from the kitchen of fate,
Seeking that goodness, oh isn't it great?
A hint of success in each savory bite,
Galloping towards glory, we savor the night.

Smoky delights with a twist of the fry,
Under the heat lamp, ambitions all lie.
With a sprinkle of laughter, we'll dive headfirst,
Chasing the aromas, quenching our thirst.

A Tantalizing Twist of Fate

Life's like a basket of potatoes divine,
Fates twist and turn, in a tasty design.
Fried to perfection, or slightly overdone,
It's all about flavor, and oh, what fun!

With tartar and humor, we slather our dreams,
Every bite a riddle, or so it seems.
In this culinary chaos, we make our own way,
As we savor each moment, with fries on display.

The Flavor of Life's Pursuits

In a world of tasty dreams,
We chase after mustard seams.
Life's a burger in disguise,
With pickles stacked high, oh my!

Grease stains on our hopeful shirts,
Onion rings are wisdoms' flirts.
We dip our fries in joy and fun,
Each bite a riddle, never done.

Ketchup for the Soul

A splash of red upon my plate,
A squeezy bottle, my fate.
Pouring smiles, it stains the heart,
With every dollop, a new start.

Tomatoes crushed in sassy ways,
Count the moments, count the days.
Life's like ketchup, thick and sweet,
With every squeeze, we find our feet.

Sifting Through the Fried Layers

Golden fries in a crispy mound,
In the crunch, our laughs abound.
Beneath the surface, secrets fry,
What's hidden deep is worth a try.

Onion rings ring out the truth,
In this diner of eternal youth.
With each bite, wisdom gets fried,
Craving answers we can't hide.

The Crunch of Consciousness

A crackle here, a crunch in thought,
In every nibble, lessons caught.
Salsa dancing on my tongue,
Life's a song that's just begun.

Bites of laughter, seasoning the day,
We munch on dreams in a playful way.
The world's a platter, stacked with thrill,
With every fry, we chase the chill.

In Pursuit of Greasy Wisdom

In shadows of the fryers' light,
I ponder life with each delight.
Ketchup dreams and mustard schemes,
Amid the crunch, I weave my themes.

Burger sages pass me by,
Pondering why the fries won't fly.
With every dip, I take a note,
Sipping soda from my moat.

Wisdom pops in golden hues,
Like crispy tales in greasy cues.
A side of jam and jelly zings,
As laughter scents the silly flings.

Whispers Between the Bites

A whisper floats from melted cheese,
As fries confess their secrets, please.
With every bite, a giggle bursts,
Unraveling thoughts that bubble first.

In pleats of paper, truths unfold,
Beneath the warmth, not all is gold.
A secret sauce, a twist of fate,
Where laughter blends on a dinner plate.

Life's queries hide in onion rings,
As I savor the joy that flavor brings.
Between the munches, insight flows,
In every crunch, my wisdom grows.

Flavor Trails and Inner Journeys

Chasing flavors like a sleuth,
Each crispy snack unveils a truth.
From ranch to BBQ, a trail,
Leading me where the good times hail.

A pizza slice with wisdom baked,
While deep-fried theories are opaque.
On wings of fries, I take my flight,
Exploring worlds past day and night.

Each condiment a guiding star,
Navigating dreams, both near and far.
In the dip lies a life profound,
Wrapped in laughter, joy unbound.

The Essence of Curly Fry Philosophy

Curly fries twist like life's surprise,
Wisdom fried in seasoned pies.
Each curl a question, crispy dance,
Inviting me to join the chance.

I twist and dip in tangy dress,
Amid potato thoughts, I guess.
Philosophers in fry baskets wait,
To share their laughs and contemplate.

From salty dreams to peppered schemes,
The essence flows through all my themes.
In fun and flavor, joy ignites,
Life's simplest treats shine brightest lights.

Thoughts Served Hot

In the café of old dreams,
I ponder my next bite,
A side of ketchup leans in,
Whispering secrets of delight.

I took a fry on a quest,
To find wisdom, not just heat,
It danced like a jester,
In its crunchy, golden seat.

Is life a combo meal?
Or perhaps a la carte?
With every dip and crunch,
I'm savoring my heart.

So pass the salt and cheer,
While I toast this grease-stained love,
For meaning served hot, dear,
Could be what I dream of.

Frying Pan Philosophies

Sizzle and pop in my mind,
Thoughts fry up without pause,
Are nuggets the truth I seek?
Or just crumbs, without cause?

In the grease of existence,
I dig for the golden fry,
Crispy covers all around,
Will I find truth? Oh my!

Now add a sprinkle of spice,
Ice cream for refining grace,
These ponderings wrap and whirl,
In a sauce of absurd place.

Philosophy with a crunch,
Life's a platter of delight,
So I'll munch through the chaos,
Until I find what's right.

Explorations in the Snack Bar of Life

Under neon lights I roam,
Through a maze of tasty treats,
With burgers like bold adventurers,
And shakes that dance to the beats.

I seek a wisdom wrapped tight,
In foil like a treasure chest,
Fries stacked high, my compass points,
To flavors I know best.

But the nachos mock my quest,
Cheesy wisdom sprinkled on,
"Dip it or lose it!" they jest,
While I ponder and yawn.

At the check-out line of dreams,
I order a side of laughs,
For meaning's just a menu,
With whimsical paragraphs.

The Texture of What Is

Crunchy edges of the truth,
Lie nestled within the fries,
Each bite a crispy riddle,
Veiled in cheesy goodbyes.

I chew on life's raw moments,
Like potatoes with great flair,
Are we mashed or just fried?
Flavorful chaos everywhere!

Onion rings, the rings of fate,
Twist and turn in greasy art,
I laugh at my flaws tonight,
With a side of dip from the heart.

Fried wisdom shared among friends,
In this snack bar, laughter flies,
With each crispy little truth,
Life's texture between the fries.

Grease-Stained Revelations

In a diner booth with a view,
I muse as ketchup drops askew,
The burger smiles like it knows,
While the fries dance in salty rows.

Life's a combo, to be fair,
Golden treasures everywhere,
With every bite, I crunch and think,
Is wisdom found in ranch orink?

Chasing dreams through greasy fumes,
Lost in thoughts while someone looms,
The waitress chuckles, gives me a wink,
Am I a thinker, or just lost in ink?

So here I sit, munching away,
Fried reflections on this tray,
A side of fries to light the way,
Perhaps that's deep? Or just cliché?

Pondering Between Fry Buckets

Amidst the crunch of potato bliss,
I sit and ponder what I miss,
Are fries the answers, crispy and hot?
Or just a snack I love a lot?

Life's choices laid in batter deep,
Do I have dreams? Or fries to keep?
Salted truths upon my plate,
Or stretchy pants to seal my fate?

Sipping shakes and pondering fries,
Are they comfort? Or just goodbyes?
I search the bottom of the bag,
For nuggets of wisdom, I must snag.

Between the bites, my mind will roam,
Can fry grease lead me to a home?
Or should I just indulge and munch,
Letting laughter take me with each crunch?

Unraveling the Seasoned Mysteries

In a world of crispy golden glow,
I wonder where my thoughts could go,
A sprinkle of salt, a dash of zest,
Seeking answers in fry-shaped quests.

Fries in a basket, secrets unfold,
Stories told by the seasoned gold,
A dip in mayo, or swipe in cheese,
What's behind this greasy tease?

Crunching through life's playful jest,
As ketchup drips, I start my quest,
Are dreams like fries, best when shared?
Or solitary snacks, slightly impaired?

With laughter bubbling like a stew,
And fries whispering, 'You know it's true,'
The mystery beckons, take a bite,
Finding joy in the silly and light.

Life's Tangles on a Plate

My plate's a mess, a colorful sight,
Ketchup rivers, fries take flight,
With every twist in the pasta's form,
Life's a swirl, never the norm.

Nuggets of wisdom sit side by side,
In crispy breading, where truths abide,
Spilling ranch on an empty slate,
Savoring fate with every plate.

A burger's smile, a pickle's frown,
Mixing flavors, upside down,
Who knew the quest for joy and taste,
Could fill my heart with gooey haste?

So here's my fortune, fried and hot,
In life's great buffet, give all that you've got,
With laughter seasoned on every bite,
It's a journey worth taking, with fries in sight.

Reflections in the Food Court

In a sea of greasy trays,
Life's choices dance in cheese.
I ponder burgers, fries, and shakes,
What's the secret that appeases?

A kid digs deep in ketchup,
While I sip on soda's fizz.
Every bite's a revelation,
It's philosophy, with a quiz.

Chicken nuggets talking loud,
Their wisdom fried to a crunch.
Do I follow my taste buds here,
Or the wellness of a brunch?

As the fryer hums its tune,
Life's truths come golden and crisp.
With each bite, I glean the joys,
In this fast-food philosophical wisp.

Flavorful Odyssey.

In the land of fries and shakes,
I search for wisdom with a smile.
Onions ring with tales to tell,
With each crispy bite, I dial.

Mayo dreams and mustard thoughts,
Like mustard seeds, they sprout.
What's the meaning of this feast?
Crunchy truths, I can't live without.

Across the counter, a burger winks,
Does it know what it brings?
Lettuce layers of deep insight,
In this meal, my heart sings.

So I down the fried delights,
With a grin, I toast my fate.
In this flavorful journey's quest,
I find the joy, I can't wait!

Fried Dreams and Philosophical Cravings

As I chew on crispy bites,
Questions bubble up like stew.
Are we more than oil and spice?
At least we all share this view.

Fries piled high like thoughts in my mind,
Dipped in ranch, they hide a tale.
The secret sauce, oh what can it be?
A paradox served with a pail.

With every crunch, a lesson learned,
Like pickles teaching me to chill.
Am I just a hungry human?
Or a philosopher with a thrill?

So here I sit, a scholar bold,
With my cup of soda pop.
In the realm of fried indulgence,
I devour truths, and don't stop!

The Quest for Crispy Clarity

In a diner filled with haze,
I seek religions made of fries.
Gravy boats guide my thoughts,
As I ponder life in disguise.

Is the milkshake a wise sage,
Or just a blend of ice and cream?
Each sip sparks an epiphany,
Like the fries, it's not what it seems.

The burger's got existential weight,
As I ponder my next great bet.
Do I savor the bun or the patty?
In this quest, I might forget.

So I laugh with a side of slaw,
In this crazy foodie cafe.
With every bite, I reach for light,
In a crispy, fried ballet.

Salted Reflections

In a diner booth, where dreams collide,
I ponder life's flavors, a side of pride.
The fries, they crunch with laughter bright,
While wisdom slips, in the neon light.

Between bites of joy and moments grand,
I dip my thoughts in a salty hand.
Each fry a nugget of sage delight,
As I munch through the dilemma of day and night.

The Hungry Quest

Off I wander, in search of fun,
With every bite, my woes come undone.
I navigate the menu with reckless glee,
Chasing fries like a wild jubilee.

The burger's laugh, the shake's wise grin,
In this greasy world, my quest begins.
I may lose my way, but I'll find my flow,
In the warmth of fries, our hearts aglow.

Deep-Fried Epiphanies

A crispy thought, like golden bliss,
Fried thoughts emerge, I can't dismiss.
As I munch on knowledge, oh so sweet,
Every fry unfolds a mystery neat.

In the batter of life, I find my role,
Seasoned with laughter, it feeds my soul.
Cheesy reflections, bubbling and bright,
Unwrap the lessons that take flight.

Whispers in the Ketchup

A dollop of red, whispers galore,
Fries and ketchup, who could ask for more?
Each dip a secret, sharing delight,
Fried friends reveal what's hidden from sight.

In the chatter of crunch, we find our way,
A symphony served on a picnic tray.
With laughter and sauce, we blaze the trail,
In this tasty pursuit, we shall not fail.

Frying Pan Philosophy

In the skillet of life, we all fry,
Sizzling thoughts drifting like a pie.
Beneath a cloud of greasy cheer,
We ponder things while munching near.

Fries in hands, we debate our fate,
Is ketchup love, or just a plate?
Hash browns whisper, cold and wise,
In this kitchen, truth may surprise.

Dreams may be crispy, soft on the inside,
With every crunch, we take a ride.
Philosophers toast with fry-laden feasts,
In this fast lane, joy never ceases.

So toss your thoughts in the hot oil whirl,
While life's soft serve begins to twirl.
With laughter seasoned like salt to fries,
We'll cook up wisdom with zest and ties.

In the Shade of Fast Food Dreams

Beneath the golden arches we sit,
Questioning life as we munch and chit.
The soft drink bubbles, the fryer hums,
In this kingdom where belly grumbles.

A burger's wisdom, wrapped and neat,
Suggests true joy is found in heat.
As fries stack high, we chew the fat,
While pondering where our dreams are at.

And in the shade of greasy lore,
We find the things we can't ignore.
A milkshake smile, a sundae sigh,
With every bite, we feel we fly.

So let's embrace this savory space,
In crispy chaos, we find our place.
From napkin wisdom, let's take a cue,
Life's a combo meal, shared by a few.

The Philosophical Potato

Oh wise potato, buried in dirt,
With layers of meaning beneath your skirt.
Fried, baked, or mashed with glee,
You ponder existence while cooking for me.

Sliced or diced, you wear many hats,
In the world of culinary spats.
Do you feel deep, or are you just fries?
What's the essence behind those eyes?

Curly or straight, you twist with fate,
You remind us how to celebrate.
In butter's glare or oil's embrace,
We find small joys in this fast-food race.

So let's emote with a potato grin,
For every meal holds a reason within.
In every crunch, laughter aligns,
With spud wisdom served with divine signs.

Slices of Existence

In a diner booth, the world is wide,
With greasy plates, we smile and bide.
Life's a pie, we slice it thin,
With every bite, where dreams begin.

Burger wraps hold secrets untold,
Hidden truths wrapped up in gold.
And fries, like thoughts, are long and real,
Crunchy insights with zest we feel.

A hotdog strolls, philosophical plight,
Mustard dreams in the neon light.
With ketchup tears and mayo grins,
We dive deep into life's whims.

So grab a seat, and let's convene,
In this weird world, nothing's routine.
With every order, we find our way,
In bites of humor, life's okay.

Between the Grease and the Grain

In a world of crispy bites,
I ponder life with sauce delights.
The burger laughs, the fries agree,
Yet wisdom's lost in calorie sea.

Whispers of ranch, secrets of cheese,
I chase my thoughts with every tease.
A milkshake slurp, a knowing grin,
Perhaps the answer's beneath this skin.

A Journey in Every Bite

Each fry a footstep, bold and brave,
Through ketchup rivers, I misbehave.
A sip of cola, a salty cheer,
Adventure waits in this dining sphere.

Onion rings swirl, like dreams gone wild,
Disguised in batter, the hopes of a child.
With every crunch, a tale unfolds,
In grease-stained glory, my fortune holds.

Deep-Fried Doubts

In a basket of fries, I find my fears,
Dip them in ranch, my laughter nears.
Is the secret sauce all that I lack?
Between bites of joy, I plan my comeback.

The nuggets of wisdom, so crispy and bright,
Deep-fried musings, served late at night.
I ponder the world, with a burger surprise,
Each bite a question, what's wise in disguise?

Tastes of Unfulfilled Dreams

The fries are golden, dreams on a plate,
I munch on wishes, is it too late?
A sprinkle of salt to season the thought,
Amidst bite after bite, my wisdom's caught.

Chasing flavors of what could have been,
With pickles of doubt, life's quirky spin.
A burger in hand, I laugh at the spread,
In this banquet of dreams, may I never be wed.

A Side of Salt and Self-Discovery

In a booth that squeaks with fate,
I ponder fries and contemplate.
Life's crispy edge, a salty bite,
What's deep in life and what's just right?

Ketchup flows like thoughts so wide,
Dip and dive, I take a ride.
Pickles whisper truths to me,
In this feast of mystery.

A burger calls, it pulls me near,
With extra cheese, I shed my fear.
Amid the crunch of life's buffet,
Fries and wisdom pave the way.

Golden Morsels of Enlightenment

Under neon lights, I sit and muse,
Fries in hand, with nothing to lose.
Golden morsels, crispy and bright,
Trying to find what's wrong and right.

Salt weighs heavy on my heart,
Is life a science or a work of art?
Dipping thoughts in ranch so cool,
Must I follow all the rules?

As I munch through every bite,
I ponder deep into the night.
Fries that shimmer, shine, and glow,
Are the secrets all below?

Contemplation with Condiments

From mustard's tang to mayo's grace,
I juggle flavors in this place.
What's the point of all this flair?
A side of souls, do we all share?

In dipping sauces, dreams are stirred,
With every bite, absurdities blurred.
A crunch, a munch, a laugh or two,
Who knew fries could teach like a guru?

To relish thoughts, or do I fry?
On this journey, I may not die.
Life's a platter, serve it right,
With every fry, shine your light.

In the Diner of Existential Questions

Sitting in a booth that creaks and groans,
I sip on cola, my mind roams.
The waitress rolls her eyes and sighs,
As I ponder life between the fries.

Are burgers fate, or just a treat?
I wrestle thoughts over something to eat.
On a plate of doubts, I find my way,
With every crunch, I seize the day.

An onion ring of twisted fate,
Do we find answers or hesitate?
In this diner of dreams and schemes,
Fries guide me through wobbly themes.

Side Plates of What Matters

In a diner booth, I ponder deep,
What makes my heart thump, awake or sleep?
Is it the ketchup, or that crispy crunch?
Or the laughs we share over a late-night lunch?

The milkshake swirls, a frosty delight,
Like dreams that bubble in the pale moonlight.
I dip my fries into thoughts so silly,
Wondering if wisdom's just as frilly!

The waiter's grin, a glimmering clue,
Smiling at fables I never knew.
Is life a combo or just a side?
With each bite I take, I'm filled with pride!

So let's toast to all that's crispy and hot,
The things that matter, or really, what's not?
In this café, with laughter and cheer,
I'll find my truth with fries and a beer!

Fables from the Fryer

In the deep fry, tales come ablaze,
Golden secrets in oil that sways.
Once I found wisdom in a cheese curd,
And a fortune wrapped tight in a burger nerd.

Salted stories that crackle and pop,
Life's little lessons that never will stop.
Each bite a mystery, each sip a song,
With friends gathered round, we can do no wrong!

Gravy dreams swirl in a saucy dance,
In this kitchen chaos, I take my chance.
Dip into laughter, spread joy on the plate,
The stories we share, they just can't wait!

So here's to the fables from fryer delight,
Where humor and hunger perfectly unite.
Let's savor each moment, dip in some cheese,
With side plates of joy, we're bound to please!

Serving Up Silent Cravings

The menu's long, my mind is a blur,
Got silent cravings, a voice in a whirr.
What do I want? A bite of this hype?
Just a side of wisdom with a crispy type!

I ask for the special, that wild surprise,
Mixed with some banter, and laughter that flies.
So many options, but what's my true need?
A slice of good fortune, or just a bit of greed?

In the corner booth, my mind takes a leap,
Fries piled high, secrets I keep.
Between bites and grins, what will I find?
A recipe for joy, or a heart that's unkind?

So serve me up crispy, with a side of delight,
In this banquet of life, let's feast through the night.
With silent cravings and a wink from above,
I'll savor each moment, wrapped in love!

Tasting Life's Mysteries

I ordered a platter of unasked questions,
With fries on the side to fuel my confessions.
The salsa's a riddle, the cheese is a jest,
In the café of life, I'm on a quest!

Each crunchy bite whispers secrets untold,
Like the laughter of friends, or adventures bold.
I sip on my soda, think deeply and wide,
With toppings of joy, I enjoy the ride!

The burger's a puzzle, the patty a clue,
Life's layered like onions, who knew?
As I chew on thoughts, the world feels at play,
Finding truths hidden in every buffet!

So here's to the feasts, and mysteries shared,
In the plates of existence, each moment is aired.
With a sprinkle of humor, I take my chance,
Tasting life's wonders in a whimsic dance!

Frying Up Philosophical Ponderings

In a world deep-fried and golden,
Questions bubble up, they're beholden.
Is ketchup the answer, or just a trap?
Drenched in decision, we take a nap.

Behold the salt, a sprinkle of doubt,
Is it the treasure we've searched about?
With each crunch, wisdom might be found,
Or just a craving, love abound.

Flip the oil, watch thoughts swim and dive,
As crispy delights make our minds thrive.
Mayonnaise of dreams, aioli of fate,
While we snack in the silence of a plate.

So grab a fry, let the laughter flow,
In every nibble, insight begins to grow.
With sprinkles of humor, we'll toast to the ride,
As we munch on our truths, side by side.

The Crunch of Truth Revealed

In the fryer of life, truth sizzles bright,
With a side of humor, we chase the light.
Beneath the crisp, the softness hides,
A silly secret that often divides.

Dipping deep in sauces, flavors collide,
Philosophy served with a side of fried.
Each bite a pondering, sweet and absurd,
Can a sweet potato fry be your next word?

Gather round, friends, with plates piled high,
Existence and laughter, oh my, oh my!
A crunch resonates, thoughts rush in twirls,
As we nibble on wisdom, a gift from the world.

In the finish, a morsel that lingers long,
Like the echo of laughter in a friendly song.
For in every fry, a dilemma lies,
Wrapped in the crunch is where the truth flies.

Unwrapping Savory Secrets

Paper wrappers hold wonders untold,
Each golden fry, a mystery bold.
On a quest for joy in a grease-stained quest,
What's deep-fried delight? We'll never rest.

Peel back the layers like a curious kid,
What's cooking inside? A thought we hid.
Burger or salad, we ponder late nights,
In the heart of the diner, life's little bites.

As we munch on the secrets, we giggle and share,
What's more profound than a warm, cheesy pair?
Life's flavors blend, in laughter they tangle,
With a side of fries, comes the perfect angle.

So unwrap your thoughts, let's take a bite,
In this comedy kitchen, everything's right.
Dipped in good humor, let worries cease,
For in every fry, we find our peace.

Life's Diner of Decisions

Late-night diners serve a plateful of choice,
Like fries on the table, they give truth a voice.
Should I dip or just salt? Decisions to make,
In every crunch, a laugh on the shake.

With menus as riddles, oh what to choose,
The burger looks lonely, should it be the muse?
A side of fries whispers secrets so bright,
They call out the questions as we munch late at night.

On the grill of existence, our thoughts feel the heat,
Saucy debates and sweet, starchy treats.
Can life be clear with chili cheese fries?
More confounding than truth in disguise.

So gather your friends for this whimsical ride,
With ketchup in hand and nothing to hide.
In the diner of life, every bite is a thrill,
For the choices we savor, they give our hearts chill.

Crunchy Contemplations

In a world of crispy dreams,
I ponder life with fries it seems.
Ketchup smiles and salty cheer,
Are these the truths I hold so dear?

Searching for wisdom in potato bliss,
What's the meaning of a cheesy kiss?
But here I munch, not quite profound,
In every bite, a joy is found.

The Salted Paradox

Fries are golden, life's just fried,
With every crunch, my thoughts collide.
Why's the world so deep, I muse,
Amidst this snack, I cannot lose?

Chasing dreams through greasy trails,
While laughing at my tiny fails.
A shake of salt, a splash of fun,
Is this a race I've truly won?

Fast Tracks to Fulfillment

With greasy hands and hopeful heart,
I dive into this fry-filled art.
Each morsel served, a lesson learned,
In every crunch, the tables turned.

Wrapped up tight in paper dreams,
With every bite, I sip the creams.
Is happiness a fried delight?
Or just a craving late at night?

Frying Up Inner Questions

Oil bubbles like my hidden thoughts,
What's wisdom worth? Are we all nuts?
As I munch on crispy goals,
Does life's meaning fry in bowls?

Dip, dunk, taste the savory round,
With laughter, my worries are drowned.
In these moments, I find my cheer,
Life's absurd, but fries are here!

The Sidewalk of Thoughts

I wander down this crowded street,
Where dreams and ketchup may just meet.
Philosophy served hot and nice,
With questions sprinkled—oh so precise.

A bump in thought—a fry falls down,
I laugh aloud and feel my frown.
A tasty snack in hand, I muse,
What's a burger without its dues?

With each crunch, new truths arise,
Like mustard's sting or onion's cries.
The sidewalks lead to insights bold,
In every bite, a story told.

So here I stroll, with salt and wit,
Finding meaning in every hit.
With laughter echoing through my mind,
A side of joy is what I find.

The Crisp Path to Understanding

On a path of golden crisp delight,
I ponder life from morning to night.
Fries are the map—each bite a clue,
With every dip, I learn something new.

A wave of grease, a hint of cheer,
I ponder why I'm even here.
The crunch of fate in a greasy sack,
Each morsel whispers, 'Don't turn back!'

With every nibble, wisdom flows,
Like pickle slices, life often slows.
I seek the sauce, the perfect blend,
For every fry becomes a friend.

And if the truths are fried and bold,
I'll munch along—this path unfolds.
There's humor found in every taste,
As I savor life, there's no time to waste.

A Crunch Above the Rest

In a diner booth, with fries galore,
I sit and ponder, ever more.
With every crunch, a thought to swell,
Crispy wisdom, who can tell?

A side of salt—a sprinkle bright,
I contemplate the day and night.
With ketchup dreams, I dip my doubt,
What's this confusion all about?

Laughter bubbles like a soda pop,
I grasp at meaning, then I stop.
To find the truth in each warm bite,
Is life a feast or just a fright?

So here I snack, my thoughts run free,
In every crunch, a mystery.
A giggle rises with each fry,
With food for thought, I'll never die!

The Essence of a Full Plate

With a full plate piled high and wide,
I munch on truths that won't subside.
Each bite a riddle, crispy and bold,
In this buffet of meat and gold.

Fries and laughter, a tasty blend,
With every nibble, I make a friend.
A side of joy, let's fill the space,
In every crunch, finding my place.

As I devour this feast of thought,
I chew on life, lessons sought.
With every fry, a giggle shared,
In this buffet, I feel prepared.

So let the ketchup flow like wine,
In every morsel, a grand design.
With full plates and spirits high,
I find my meaning—one fry at a time!

Fryers and Fables

In a pan of bubbling dreams,
We toss our thoughts like spuds,
Golden tales in crispy seams,
Life's a feast, we'll skip the duds.

With ketchup smiles, we dip and dive,
Each fry a story on our tongue,
In this world, we come alive,
While laughter sings, we're forever young.

A sprinkle of salt, a dash of cheer,
We season woes with every bite,
In this banquet, we show no fear,
Dancing fries, a tasty sight.

So here's to tales both old and new,
Fryers bubbling, laughter flows,
With crispy dreams and friends like glue,
In this kitchen of life, anything goes.

The Essence on the Plate

On porcelain dreams, we pile our fate,
With crispy edges that narrate,
Life's absurdity, a golden state,
Each bite a giggle, never late.

A sprinkle of humor, a dash of zest,
With every crunch, we're put to the test,
Can fries indeed be the very best?
Oh yes, they're way better than the rest!

A side of joy, a dollop of fun,
In every basket, a treasure spun,
We feast on laughter, the heart has won,
With fries in hand, life's never done.

So what's the secret, the essence divine?
It's sharing fries, over the line,
In every bite, a sunny sign,
Together we sparkle, like vintage wine.

A Taste of Tomorrow

Each fry a promise, a delicate jest,
We savor the moments, we feel so blessed,
In tomorrow's crunch, we're put to the test,
With laughter and spices, life's a fest.

Dipped in dreams, our futures fry,
A sweet surprise, oh me, oh my,
With each golden piece, we lift and fly,
To flavors unknown, we touch the sky.

No worries simmer, no griefs to stew,
Just crispy delights and flavors anew,
In this kitchen of laughs, we all pursue,
The taste of tomorrow, me and you.

So here's to fries, those whimsical friends,
They season our lives, the fun never ends,
With every dip, the joy transcends,
In this savory tale, our hearts we lend.

Once Upon a Side Dish

In a tale where fries take the lead,
Once upon a time, in a kitchen of greed,
A crispy adventure, oh what a need,
With laughter and spice, we spread the seed.

Each fry a character, with stories to tell,
In the warmth of a fryer, all's well,
Dancing with joy, under a golden spell,
They bring out the giggles, oh can't you tell?

So here's to the moments, the savory thrill,
With every side dish, we chase the chill,
In a world so wild, we fry at will,
For laughter and fries, we all shall fill.

And if ever you ponder, the meaning of fries,
Look to your heart, where the laughter lies,
In crispy tales and friendship ties,
Once upon a side dish, wisdom flies.

Undercurrents of Flavorful Inquiry

In a diner booth, my mind takes flight,
Ketchup dreams and mayo thoughts ignite.
The universe whispers from the fryer's hum,
A side of wisdom, served hot and dumb.

With each crunch, I ponder life's deep quest,
Are we but nuggets, or are we the best?
Salted secrets tumble from my plate,
As I dip my questions in fate's open gate.

What do we crave in this buffet of fate?
Is it love, success, or a burger plate?
The shake of laughter, a sprinkle of glee,
In every fry, I find parts of me.

Through cheesy layers, I slice through the night,
Eating my thoughts under neon light.
In this feast of whims, we dance and play,
A flavorful journey, come what may.

Soul Snacks and Thought Bites

A basket of dreams, golden and bold,
Every bite tells a story untold.
Craving the essence that brings us alive,
In a world of snacks, we learn to thrive.

Between crispy bits, our laughter resides,
Life's savory moments, in closeness, collides.
Are we fries with sprinkles of joy so bright?
Or just plain potatoes lost in the night?

With honey mustard, I ponder the wise,
Are burdens just spuds dressed up in disguise?
Tater tots twinkle, a clue here and there,
In each crunchy morsel, a thought's tender care.

So I dip and I dive in this platter of light,
Flavors of friendship, making wrongs feel right.
With nachos and giggles, my mind's on a spree,
These soul snacks remind me of what it means to be free.

Crispy Questions with a Side of Silence

In the still of fries, I hear whispers call,
Are we just snacks at this grand buffet ball?
With every crunch, do we unveil the tease,
Or are we just chasing a savory breeze?

What if the ketchup holds secrets galore,
And every potato knows the path to explore?
With a side of silence, I lean back and muse,
In this crispy question, I'll take the good news.

Do burgers have dreams, or is it all a jest?
Is the pickle a sage, wise and well-dressed?
Fries stack the wonders, a tower of taste,
In every byte ponder all illusions laid waste.

As I dip my thoughts in a creamy delight,
I ponder existence in buttery light.
In this fast-food heaven, I wrangle my mind,
With crispy questions, the answers unwind.

A Palette of Possibilities

In a diner of whims, I paint with my fries,
Dipped in curiosity, sprinkled with sighs.
A palette of options, so colorful, bright,
In every bite, I discover my light.

What if the burger could tell me it's true,
That deep-fried moments give flavor anew?
With layers of laughter and swirls of delight,
I'm tasting the cosmos in each little bite.

Fries in a row, like thoughts in my mind,
Each crunchy reflection, a treasure to find.
In the freedom of grease, we dance with the night,
A canvas of chaos, a delicious flight.

So pass me the sauce, I'll layer on cheer,
As I ponder the questions that bring me near.
In my plate of laughter, I see the unseen,
A palette of life, where I'm bold and serene.

Dipping into Desire

In a world that fries and sizzles,
I ponder my crispy dreams.
The ketchup whispers sweet nothings,
While pickles scheme like beams.

Mayo carries my hopes,
A tangy twist in the air.
With each dip, I ask, why not?
Life's better with flair!

Fries dance in a warm embrace,
On my plate, they tease and twirl.
Oh, the joys of salty bliss,
In this fry-filled, foodie whirl.

So I laugh with my side dish bright,
As laughter meets a crunchy bite.
In every fry, a question stirs,
Underneath those crispy slurs.

Musing Over Order Up

At the counter, I stand in line,
With a menu that slips my mind.
What's life without a side of fries?
A craving I cannot unwind.

The soda fizzes with delight,
As I thumb through thoughts unspoken.
Do burgers know their own worth?
Or is it just fries that are broken?

The waitress grins, my heart skips,
Does she know my secret yearning?
With every order, I question fate,
Like the oil that keeps on churning.

As I munch with glee and cheer,
In this feast, my doubts disappear.
With every crunch and tasty bite,
I ponder order in sheer delight.

Battered Thoughts and Saucy Reflections

In this diner, thoughts get battered,
As I munch with a side of sass.
Who needs deep philosophy,
When fries are here to pass?

Each crunch a revelation bright,
And dip brings juicy lore.
The world feels lighter in this chair,
I've found my forever score!

Gravy pools like lost ideas,
While cheese plays hide and seek.
Are they flavors of life's path?
Or tangy tricks, unique?

With a smirk, I raise my cup,
Life's a contrast, sweet and tough.
In the grease, my heart finds ease,
In laughter, serving up enough.

The Simmering Questions of the Heart

In a pot of bubbling oil,
I wonder about love's heat.
Do fries know their destiny?
Or do they drown in the sweet?

What if dips had secrets deep,
From ranch to spicy bar?
Would they spill their guts to me,
Or simply say, "Here we are!"

With every side I ponder life,
In this cozy, fried-up place.
Are our choices just like toppings,
Or the fries' lost, crispy grace?

So in this diner here tonight,
With each bite, I play my part.
For in laughter and in fries,
I uncover my fool's heart.

The Quest Beyond the Condiments

In a world where ketchup flows,
Mustard joins the playful shows.
Our fries dance on the table's edge,
As we debate the veggie pledge.

With burger knights and soda queens,
We ride on waves of salty dreams.
Nuggets whisper secrets deep,
While coleslaw guards our belly's keep.

Oh, relish, what do you propose?
Shall we dive into a pickle knows?
Fries our compass, sauces our chart,
Adventure's spark ignites the heart.

So let's embark, let laughter swell,
In this fast-food wonderland, we dwell.
A treasure trove of taste awaits,
With crispy friends on our dinner plates.

Golden Expectations

Fries of gold like dreams unfold,
In a basket, stories told.
Each crunchy bite, a joy parade,
In the fast-food sun, we're unafraid.

We're fry-crusaders, bold and bright,
Chasing snack myths, a wondrous sight.
With every dip, we laugh and cheer,
These golden wonders, oh so dear.

On potato clouds, our hopes take flight,
As we munch under neon lights.
A side of giggles, a dash of fun,
In this greasy kingdom, we've all won.

So here's to fries, crispy and hot,
Life's little moments that hit the spot.
With friends beside and laughter loud,
In golden expectations, we're forever proud.

Beyond the Box of Takeout

A carton brimming, treasures lie,
Fries peek out, oh my, oh my!
With every crunch, the world ignites,
In greasy glories, we find delights.

Egg rolls prompt a daring chase,
While onion rings join the embrace.
We venture forth, forks in hand,
Exploring flavors, bold and grand.

Together we unwrap the fate,
A feast that makes us celebrate.
Like hidden gems, the dips unfold,
In this culinary tale, we're bold.

Oh takeout box, what dreams you hold,
With every bite, the stories told.
We laugh and munch through endless nights,
Adventurers in these tasty heights.

Twilight Taste Adventures

As twilight falls on fry-filled streets,
We savor adventures, our joyous feats.
Ketchup rivers, a tart surprise,
Under a sky of glowing fries.

Soda fountains, we take the leap,
To find what stirs in bowls so deep.
Mysteries unfold with each crisp bite,
In this kooky, culinary night.

Fries like stars in greasy skies,
Make us giggle, fuel our highs.
In every crunch, a world unexplored,
With laughter as our greatest sword.

So let's unite, in laughter's glow,
As we dance with fries, let good vibes flow.
From twilight's start to that last fry,
In tasty fun, we'll soar and fly.

Dining with the Inner Self

A table set for one, oh what a sight,
With burgers piled high, my inner thoughts take flight.
Fries scattered like dreams upon the plate,
I ponder life's meaning while I contemplate.

The ketchup smiles back, a red, saucy cheer,
As I munch on my doubts, they're less severe.
With each crunchy bite, I laugh at my fate,
Is it wrong to think I articulate my plate?

The soda bubbles softly, like a thoughtful muse,
In this greasy kingdom, I can't refuse.
Between bites of wisdom, my fries disappear,
Am I learning or just filling up on beer?

Oh, culinary guide, lead me to the fun,
Where deep-fried lessons are surely well done.
As I dine with myself, what a splendid delight,
I leave with a smile, feeling just right.

Crinkle-Cut Contemplations

In a diner booth with a view of the fry,
I ponder on life while I nibble and sigh.
Crinkle-cut dreams twirl on a plate,
Like thoughts wandering 'round, it's never too late.

Salted ideas fall like rain from the sky,
Each bite's a reminder of how time can fly.
I laugh at the whispers of fries in a heap,
Their crispy confessions make me lose sleep.

With every dip in ranch, my worries do fade,
These crispy companions make my thoughts cascade.
Onions ring softly, they join in the fun,
Together we ponder until the meal's done.

So, I take a moment, amidst all the grease,
To find a bit of comfort, a slice of peace.
A diner's divine, where the fry magic lies,
In the crispy embrace, let's open our eyes.

Flavors of Infinity on a Plate

In a world full of flavors, I'm lost but not scared,
Each bite tells a story, I'm thrilled and prepared.
Beneath the soft cheese, vast notions reside,
With fries as my compass, I'll swallow my pride.

A milkshake of wisdom, whipped up so nice,
With cherries on top, who needs to think twice?
Each sip brings reflections, frothy and bright,
As I chew on my thoughts in the neon-loud night.

Pondering sweet ketchup, so tangy and bold,
Offers morsels of meaning just waiting to unfold.
Like a burger stacked high, my ideas dare grow,
While crinkle-cut bites tell me all that I know.

With fries by my side, I'm never alone,
In this feast of existence, my heart finds a home.
Where flavors collide, I'll journey and sway,
In the café of life, chasing fries every day.

Savory Conversations with the Self

With a plate of temptation, I speak with my gut,
Fries crackle and whisper, while I ponder what's up.
A burger's deep secrets are tucked in each layer,
As I savor the jokes and the laughter I may share.

The veggie struggle shows up on the side,
Trying hard to fit in, it just can't decide.
While I munch on my fries, what wisdom to glean?
Do I really need veggies to find out what's green?

Amidst the light banter of relish and buns,
I tumble through life like a child when it runs.
Each dip of the fry speaks of joy and of woe,
My inner self chuckles—oh, how much I grow!

So let's share this meal, just me and my plate,
In fries we trust, let's not hesitate.
A feast for the heart, while we deepen the chat,
With savory companions, imagine that!

www.ingramcontent.com/pod-product-compliance
Lightning Source LLC
Chambersburg PA
CBHW051657160426
43209CB00004B/929